Published 1992 by Thomasson-Grant, Inc.
Copyright © 1991 by Ediciones Destino, S.A.,
Barcelona, Spain

Printed in Spain

99 98 97 96 95 94 93 92   5 4 3 2 1

Library of Congress
Cataloging-in-Publication Data

Capdevilla i Valls, Roser
      [Jugemos a contar. English]
      Let's Count! / illustrations by Roser Capdevila; text by
Elisabet Ballart.
            p. cm.
      Translation of: Jugemos a contar.
      Summary: Animals in various groupings provide count-
ing practice for the reader and introduce the idea of sets
and subsets.
      ISBN 1-56566-011-0
      [1. Animals—Fiction. 2. Stories in rhyme. 3. Counting.]
I. Ballart, Elisabet. II. Title.
PZ8.3.C193Le 1992
[E]—dc20   92-2813
                                                CIP
                                                AC

THOMASSON-GRANT
One Morton Drive
Charlottesville, Virginia 22901
804-977-1780

LET'S COUNT!

Illustrations by
Roser Capdevila

Text by
Elisabet Ballart

THOMASSON-GRANT

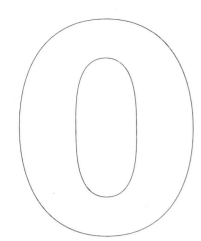

Mrs. Sheep says, "Class, let's have some fun.
Today we'll practice counting—begin with ONE."

TWO pigs in love are blushing with pride
When the minister says, "You may kiss the bride."

THREE busy monkeys in a construction crew
May make quite a mess before the work is through.

FOUR parrots practice for their first big show.
The singer sings high, the cello plays low.

FIVE tired ducks dressed for a hard day's work
Will travel by plane all the way to New York.

6

SIX medical rabbits must really be quick
To care for all the bunnies who are hurt or sick.

SEVEN dogs at the deli choosing sausage and bones
Load up their baskets before heading for home.

7

8

EIGHT cats practice for the big mile race.
A yummy fish supper is the prize for first place.

NINE mice twirl and whirl around in a dance.
They'll become ballerinas if they get the chance.

10

TEN kindergarten lambs think the first day is scary.
The littlest one is crying—she misses her friend Mary.

ELEVEN sheep are ready for the first roll call.
Little Charlie won't go anywhere without his yellow ball.

12

Becky lamb was hurt when she fell with a boom.
Now there are TWELVE in Mrs. Sheep's room.

13

All the lambs but one think recess is great.
Now there are THIRTEEN–Why is Billy so late?

14

FOURTEEN sheep wait in the bathroom line.
It looks as if one didn't make it in time.

FIFTEEN sheep take a break at lunch,
All of them hungry for something to munch.

16

SIXTEEN sheep keep fit and stay trim.
Each takes a turn leading class in the gym.

SEVENTEEN sheep at music time
Play their flutes and sing in rhyme.

17

18

Swimming class ends each day at school.
EIGHTEEN sheep gather around the pool.

19

Now there are NINETEEN—we've counted each one.
It's time to pack up—the school day is done.

Why do TWENTY guests need a cake so big?
It's easy to guess—the party's for pigs!

Masons, painters, and plasterers, THIRTY in all,
These monkeys at work are having a ball.

FORTY parrots enjoy a concert that lasts for hours. The singer takes a bow with a bouquet of flowers.

FIFTY ducks at the airport get ready to fly.
Most seem happy, but two are sad to say good-bye.

SIXTY bunnies gather in the hospital nursery.
Mother rabbit's having babies—what a big family.

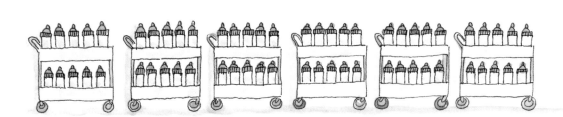

These dogs are buying groceries and meeting with their friends.
Can you see that SEVENTY is seven groups of ten?

On the day of the race EIGHTY cats fill the park,
But they'd all run away at the sound of a bark.

80

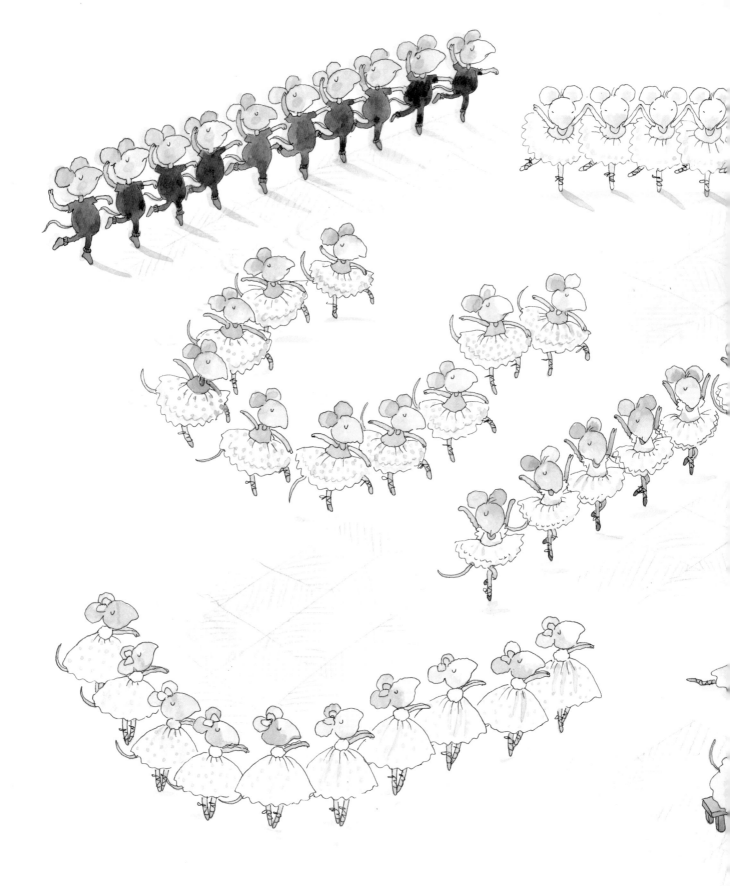

NINETY mouse dancers rise up on their toes,
Gracefully moving in nine equal rows.

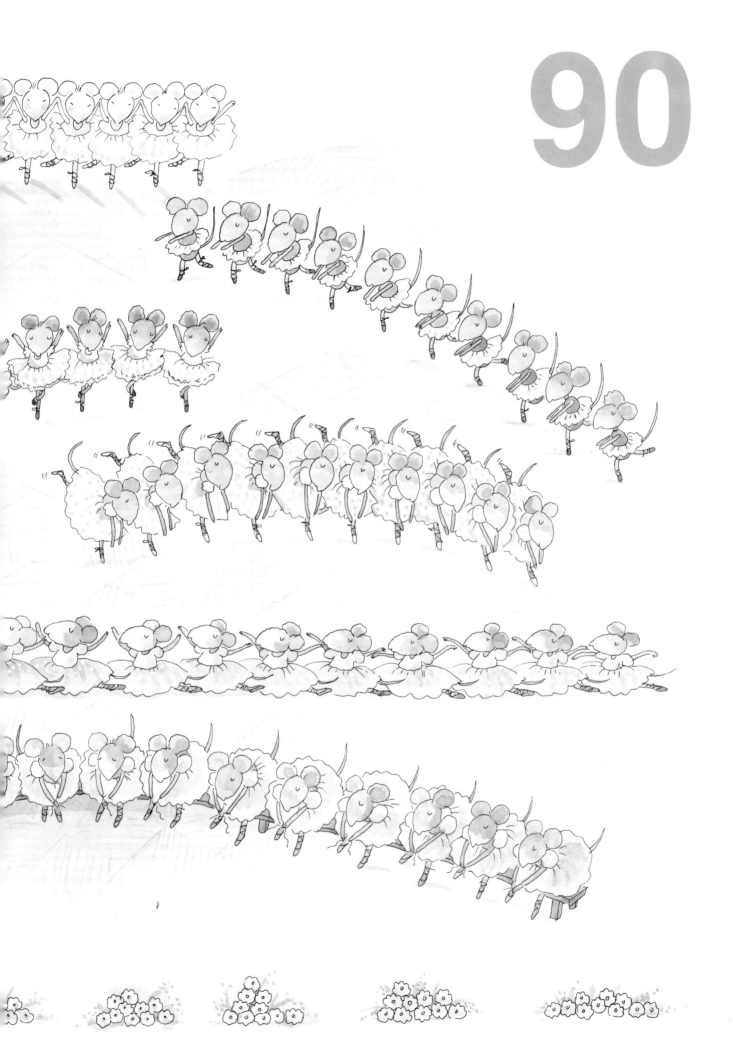

90

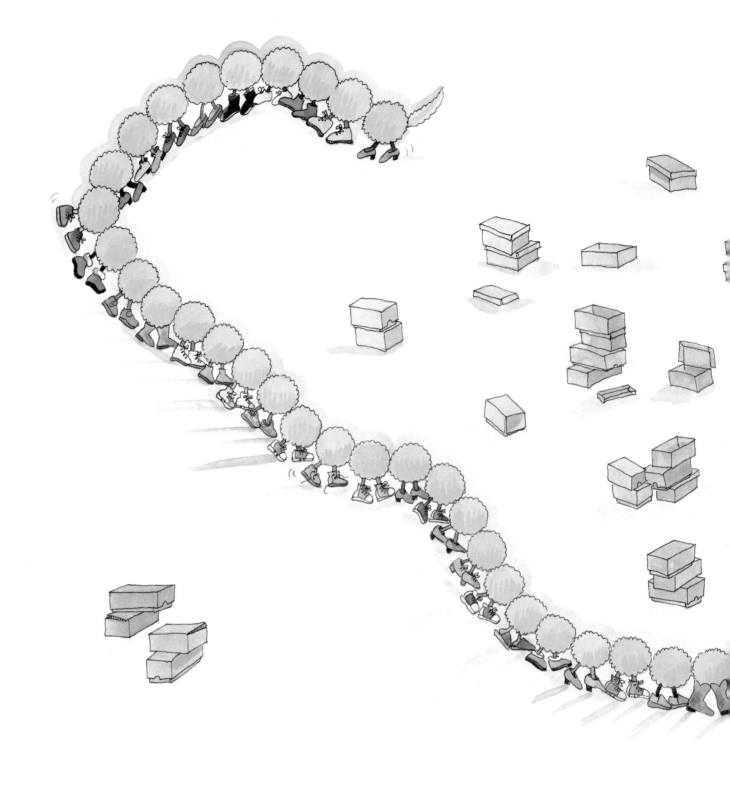

A centipede tries on ONE HUNDRED shoes.
About left and right, he is slightly confused.

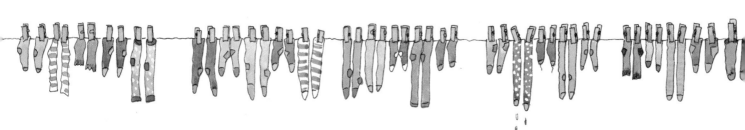

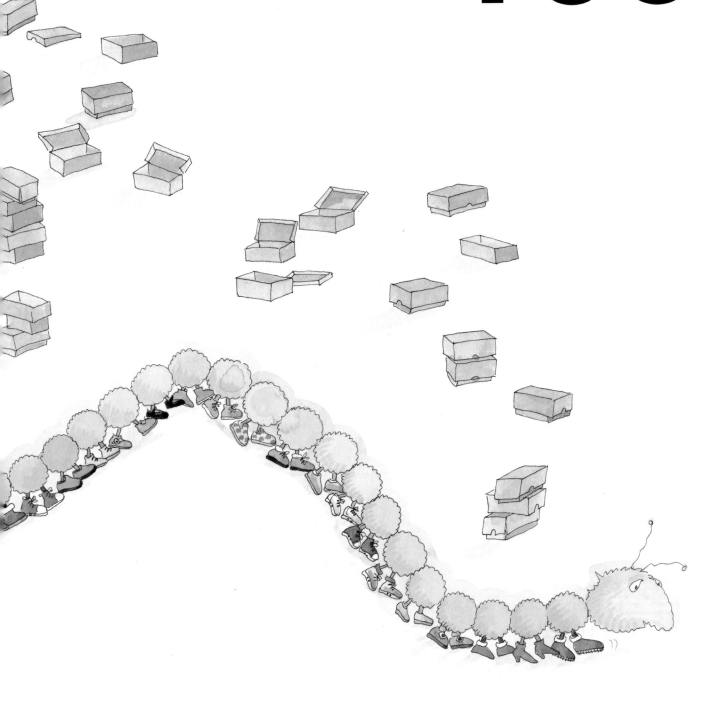

FOR MORE COUNTING FUN. . .

Once you have counted from zero to one hundred,
go back to each page and look again.

Beginners can enjoy exploring each picture
and getting to know all the characters.

For extra practice, there are objects
to be counted at the foot of each page–
five airplanes, twelve notebooks, sixty baby bottles.

For even more fun, characters and objects
appear in groups of five and ten.
In the page with thirty monkeys, for example,
there are ten plasterers in white hats,
ten painters in red hats,
and ten masons in yellow hats.
Each page has many such groups–
see what you can find!